IMAGES OF WAR

HITLER'S ORDER POLICE 1936–42

RARE PHOTOGRAPHS FROM WARTIME ARCHIVES

Ian Baxter

Pen & Sword
MILITARY

First published in Great Britain in 2025 by
PEN & SWORD MILITARY
an imprint of Pen & Sword Books Ltd
Yorkshire – Philadelphia

ISBN 978-1-03611-772-6

A CIP catalogue record for this book is available from the British Library.

Typeset by Concept, Huddersfield, West Yorkshire, HD4 5JL.
Printed and bound in England by CPI Group (UK) Ltd, Croydon, CR0 4YY.

The Publisher's authorised representative in the EU for product safety is Authorised Rep Compliance Ltd, Ground Floor, 71 Lower Baggot Street, Dublin D02 P593, Ireland – www.arccompliance.com

For a complete list of Pen & Sword titles please contact
PEN & SWORD BOOKS LTD
47 Church Street, Barnsley, South Yorkshire, S70 2AS, England
E-mail: enquiries@pen-and-sword.co.uk
Website: www.pen-and-sword.co.uk
or
PEN & SWORD BOOKS
1950 Lawrence Road, Havertown, PA 19083, USA
E-mail: uspen-and-sword@casematepublishers.com
Website: www.penandswordbooks.com

Contents

Introduction 5

Chapter One
Prelude to Terror 7

Chapter Two
Poland 21

Chapter Three
Ghettos 41

Chapter Four
Russia 1941–42 63

Chapter Five
Other Areas of Operations 1939–42 83

Appendix
Order Police Battalions 111

About the Author

Ian Baxter is a military historian who specialises in German twentieth-century military history. He has written more than seventy books, including *Poland: The Eighteen-Day Victory March*; *Panzers in North Africa*; *The Waffen-SS Ardennes Offensive*; *The Western Campaign*; *The 12th SS Panzer Division Hitlerjugend*; *Waffen-SS on the Western Front*; *Waffen-SS on the Eastern Front*; *The Red Army at Stalingrad*; *Elite German Forces of World War II*; *Armoured Warfare: German Tanks of World War II*; *Blitzkrieg*; *Panzer Divisions at War*; *German Armoured Vehicles of World War Two*; *Last Two Years of the Waffen-SS at War*; *German Soldier Uniforms and Insignia*; *German Guns of the Third Reich*; *From Retreat to Defeat: The Last Years of the German Army at War 1943–45* and, most recently, *The Sixth Army and the Road to Stalingrad*.

He has written over a hundred articles, including 'Last days of Hitler', 'Wolf's Lair', 'The Story of the V1 and V2 Rocket Programme', 'Secret Aircraft of World War Two', 'Rommel at Tobruk', 'Hitler's War with his Generals', 'Secret British Plans to Assassinate Hitler', 'The SS at Arnhem', 'Hitlerjugend', 'Battle of Caen 1944', 'Gebirgsjäger at War', 'Panzer Crews', 'Hitlerjugend Guerrillas', 'Last Battles in the East', 'The Battle of Berlin' and many more.

He has also reviewed numerous military studies for publication, supplied thousands of photographs and important documents to various publishers and film production companies worldwide, and he lectures to schools, colleges and universities throughout the United Kingdom and the Republic of Ireland.

Introduction

The *Ordnungspolizei* (Order Police or *Orpo*) was one of the main forces used for the security of Nazi Germany. During the 1930s Heinrich Himmler, head of the SS, along with the commander-in-chief of the Order Police Kurt Daluege totally reconstructed the police force of the Weimar Republic into a number of strong militarized formations. Those who served in this new police force were more than ready to carry out any task asked of them by the Nazis including the persecution of Jews and anyone deemed to be inferior by the Nazi regime. In fact in 1938 police units participated in the annexation of Austria and the occupation of Czechoslovakia. A year later when Germany invaded Poland, the role of the police changed forever. Police units were deployed alongside the German military including the special units of the *Einsatzgruppen* (death squads). In Poland Order Police were transformed into militarized police battalions and participated in combat operations which included carrying out security duties behind enemy lines. These duties were often sinister and alongside some Wehrmacht, *Waffen-SS* and *Einsatzgruppen* the police battalions engaged in the systematic murder and annihilation of Poles and Jews.

Following the conquest of Poland, the Nazi leadership created a massive recruitment drive conscripting more than 95,000 men in their thirties. A further 26,000 younger men were also recruited and indoctrinated into Nazi ideology and trained for combat.

These new recruits would now take part not only in military operations, but would also be an integral part of the Holocaust responsible for mass murders and guarding some of the Jewish ghettos. They would also assist in the destruction of the ghettos and help in the deportation transports of Jews to the concentration camps. During the summer of 1941 these police units were involved in the mass killings of Babi Yar, Rumbula and Stanislaviv. Yet after the war many of the Order Policemen claimed never to have been involved in Nazi crimes.

Chapter One

Prelude to Terror

In June 1936, chief of the SS Heinrich Himmler was formally named chief of the German police, and he reorganized the previous uniformed law enforcement agency into what was known as the *Ordnungspolizei*. Its main office was run by officers of the SS. The German police were divided into the new Order Police and the *Sicherheitspolizei* (*SiPo* or Security Police), which had been created in June 1936.

The *Orpo* operated its police units for regular uniformed law enforcement, while the *SiPo* was a secret state police force known as the *Geheime Staatspolizei* (Gestapo) including the criminal investigation police known as the *Kriminalpolizei* or *Kripo*.

During the late 1930s the *Orpo* grew considerably in size and remained under the direct control of Himmler from the central command office known as the *Hauptamt Ordnungspolizei* located in Berlin. This office, which was led by Chief of the Order Police (*Chef der Ordnungspolizei*) Kurt Daluege, was responsible for implementing and ordering the *Orpo* onto a war footing during the summer of 1939. Himmler wanted units of the *Orpo* to be converted into military formations with the men trained and outfitted by the main police offices across Germany.

The *Orpo* were formed into *Polizei* battalions and each battalion comprised some 500 men who were armed with light infantry weapons. Generally these police battalions would not be involved in front-line battle duties, but would follow the advancing Wehrmacht forces into enemy territory and undertake a more sinister role in operations. Although the many policemen at the time had continued to carry out their normal duties including traffic regulation, order maintenance and crime prevention, their function as a regular police force was about to change. Every man was to undergo Nazification and become aligned with the ideals of the Nazi regime so that the police could fulfil their new role in the East.

In order for the men of the *Orpo* to undertake such menacing duties in Poland, during their training Himmler had made it clear to Daluege that his police force should be radicalized for war. It was important, he said, to Nazify the Order Police. As a result of this policy he demanded blind and absolute obedience and that the enemy should be treated with fanatical hatred. This included learning about enemies of the state and the men's indoctrination into SS philosophy and racial superiority. Himmler assumed that these ideological teachings would result in men who ardently believed in the new Aryan order. Many of the recruits and reservists, often young, fanatical Nazis, were trained and led by experienced Order Policemen. Quite typically the police units comprised young recruits in their twenties who did not want to serve in the army, but who hoped to build a career within the police force instead. Himmler saw this as a prime opportunity and believed that the new recruits would be susceptible to anti-Semitic propaganda. In his view, once these recruits had been indoctrinated in their belief in the Aryan order which included the main fascist ideology of enslavement, extermination and ethnic persecution they would be ready to police the captured rear territories without compunction. This would include anti-Jewish violence.

Training was not as extensive or as hard as for the military, and although the recruits and reservists still undertook normal police activities, the main focus of their schooling was Nazi ideology and training for combat. All the men were told to show particular hatred towards the Jews. Frequently the recruits listened while their commanders brazenly delivered lectures about who they considered to be the most dangerous enemies of National Socialism. They instructed the police to be predominantly brutal with the Jews and use whatever violence was deemed necessary.

By August 1939 the *Orpo* comprised some 17 battalions totalling approximately 8,500 men. Administratively they remained under the command of Police Chief Daluege, but operationally they were under the direct authority of regional SS and police leaders who all reported up a separate chain of command to SS leader Himmler. For operations against Poland, the SS planned to use the police battalions in a variety of roles including various auxiliary duties comprising anti-partisan operations in support of advancing troops in the rear areas of the conquered territories. Other battalions would be given more traditional security roles as an occupying force, while others were directly ordered to be involved in more disturbing actions such as operating both independently and in conjunction with killing operations in the rear areas with the *Einsatzgruppen*, the special task forces that travelled in the wake of the German armies and would murder people by mass shooting and gassing. These task forces were created from an ad hoc *Einsatzkommando* and were responsible for securing government buildings and documents. Originally these *Einsatzkommando truppen* were part of the *Sicherheitspolizei*. Now, along with numerous battalions of the *Orpo*, they would play an integral part in genocide on an unprecedented scale.

A policeman in Berlin during early 1939. Hitler and Göring both believed that the police would have a very important role to play in Nazi Germany. For this reason they implemented a number of measures to free the police from the Weimar constitution. They also encouraged the police to target the Nazis' political opponents such as communists and Social Democrats.

A policeman supported by a brown-shirted SA stormtrooper marches along a road with a police dog. Within weeks of Hitler coming to power Göring began calling on members of the SS, SA and *Stahlhelm* (a nationalist veterans' organization) as *Hilfspolizei* (auxiliary policemen) in many German states.

A Weimar policeman searches a regular SA stormtrooper, most probably prior to a Nazi rally. By 1934 the SA had grown considerably in size and was regard by Chief of Police SS Heinrich Himmler as a threat to the Nazi regime and the SS itself. It was therefore important to reduce the size of the SA, and initially this began with recruiting SA men into the police.

A photograph taken on 3 March 1933 showing local German police searching a messenger for a social democratic newspaper. Initially the chief of the German police when Adolf Hitler came to power was the Minister of the Interior, Wilhelm Frick, who along with Hermann Göring exercised executive power over Germany's police departments.

A small group of Jewish men who had been rounded up for arrest in the days after *Kristallnacht* ('the Night of Broken Glass') file out of the police station in Stadthagen escorted by German police and SA members. After Hitler came to power Nazi police leaders began changing police traditions to align with Nazi values. In early 1934 there were celebrations called 'The Day of the German Police' honouring the connection between the police and the people. *(United States Holocaust Memorial Museum – USHMM)*

Police force a group of men who were regarded as political opponents of the Nazis to crouch with their arms out, which was a form of torture. Those that collapsed were often beaten. Many would be taken away and either interrogated in police headquarters or sent to concentration camps.

A small group of Jews who had been rounded up for arrest after *Kristallnacht* are being escorted down a street by German police, SA and SS members. *(United States Holocaust Memorial Museum – USHMM)*

Two photographs taken in sequence. After being forced to clean the streets, this Jewish victim of Nazi harassment tries to resist the SA men who force him to push the supply cart down the street.
(United States Holocaust Memorial Museum – USHMM)

Austrian police stand guard outside a Jewish-owned business damaged in terror bombing by Austrian Nazis. *(United States Holocaust Memorial Museum – USHMM)*

German Police Chief *SS-Gruppenführer* Kurt Daluege (right), Heinrich Lankenau and Adolf von Bomhard at Bremen during a meeting on 23 April 1937. Daluege was an SS and police official who served as chief of the *Ordnungspolizei* (Order Police) from 1936 to 1943.

The first of two portrait photographs of Police Chief Kurt Daluege taken in 1936.

Daluege cooperated in transforming the police force of the Weimar Republic into various militarized units ready to serve the Nazis' aims of domination and racial eradication.

Himmler, Heydrich, Daluege and Adolf Hühnlein at a memorial ceremony on German Police Day, Horst-Wessel-Platz, Berlin, Germany on 16 January 1937.

Two photographs taken in sequence taken on 23 April 1937 showing Daluege, Lankenau and Bomhard inspecting a police force in Bremen. Before the war the Order Police were generally a Nazi law enforcement agency and an emergency response organization tasked with various fire brigade, coast guard and civil defence duties.

Daluege at a German police riding school in Rathenow, Germany on 2 November 1938. The Order Police wearing green uniforms were nicknamed the *Grüne Polizei* (the green police). They were first established as a centralized organization operating in various towns and cities.

Daluege at a Nazi Party rally with other police officers at Nuremberg, Germany on 6 September 1938.

Chapter Two

Poland

On 1 September 1939 the Germans launched their invasion of Poland Directive No. 1 and code-named 'Case White' (*Fall Weiss*). While the Luftwaffe bombed key Polish bridges together with cities and towns across Poland, on the ground the Wehrmacht attacked the Polish army with two army groups: Army Group North consisting of the Fourth and Third armies and Southern Army Group consisting of the Eighth, Tenth and Fourteenth armies. The entire thrust of the German army was very swift; the fast and devastating blitzkrieg had arrived.

Alongside the Wehrmacht forces Himmler's military arm of the SS-VT (later the *Waffen-SS*) was also launched into combat for the first time. However, a more menacing force was soon released into the rear areas of Poland and these were the SS Death's Head groups or *SS-Totenkopfverbände* under the notorious command of Theodor Eicke. Three regiments had been deployed: SS *Oberbayern*, *Brandenburg* and *Thuringen*. These soldiers were the *Einsatzgruppen* SS paramilitary death squads.

To support the ground invasion of Poland the Order Police were given specific orders that a number of battalions would participate in operations in the rear in order to police and suppress local resistance. This 'Jewish question in the occupied territory' went to the chiefs of all police and *Einsatzgruppen*, who were given implicit orders to round up all the Jewish people in Poland with the intention of placing them into holding areas for ghettos. However, in reality the plans were more barbaric than just rounding up those they regarded as hostile to the Reich. The mission of the police and the *Einsatzgruppen* through Poland would be to kill members of the Polish leadership. This would include the intelligentsia, teachers, the clergy and the nobility. Using dossiers collected by the SD, lists were drawn up of people to be killed in Poland. Part of this list included members of Polish society such as Jews, prostitutes, Romani people and the mentally ill. For this action the *Einsatzgruppen* along with auxiliary personnel, SS and police battalions were tasked not with employing their military capabilities, but instead terrorizing the civilian population through acts that included hunting down straggling Polish soldiers, confiscating livestock and agricultural produce, and torturing and murdering large numbers of Polish political leaders, businessmen, priests, intellectuals and Jews.

As soon as these forces were released into the rear areas the units quickly gained a reputation, and in a matter of days they began eradicating the Poles by means of torture and murder. By the end of the campaign in Poland, it was also estimated that some 531 towns and villages had been burned.

In order to secure the rear areas the police battalions would become an integral part of these barbaric operations. Police Battalion I/1, which had been formed during early September 1939 and was made up of regular policemen and reservists, were told that they would be transported to operate in the rear areas of Poland where the German 14th Army was operating. When the battalion arrived in southern Silesia German forces had already secured large areas of captured territory. It was here that the battalion was instructed to inflict harsh treatment on the Jewish population and 'force them to leave the country'. However, when the police arrived in various towns and villages they carried out a number of executions, arrests and also set fire to a number of synagogues. Following the capture of Kraków, Tarnów and Przemyśl they were ordered to arrest whoever they considered to be partisans. What followed were the shootings of Jews and Poles that had showed some resistance to the invading German forces.

While these barbaric actions were being undertaken Police Battalion II/1 followed the *Einsatzgruppen* in the Katowice/Kattowitz area of the German 14th Army and inflicted violence against both Jewish and Polish communities. In the same area of operations Police Battalion III/1 was ordered to pacify the local area around the town of Osświęcim (later Auschwitz). It carried out numerous operations including reconnaissance patrols with the 13th Armoured Company. These units roamed the countryside and performed summary executions within local Jewish areas. This included the shooting of women and children, setting fire to synagogues and forcing terrified Jewish people to flee across the Polish border.

Numerous other police battalions were also involved in indiscriminate murders of Jews and Poles in the rear areas. These comprised Police Battalions IV/1, V/1 and I/2 which operated in the rear areas of the German 10th Army. Police Battalion II/2 was given instructions to round up Polish PoWs, collect abandoned Polish battlefield booty and guard the prisoners. However, it was also involved in performing a reprisal massacre of several hundred Polish people for what it considered was 'the murder of German soldiers'.

Police Battalion III/2 was also another police unit that took part in rounding up Polish prisoners in the German 10th Army area. It was involved in a series of executions of Polish prisoners including captured Polish soldiers. However, a number of policemen, especially some of the older men, refused to take part in these murders.

Police Battalions IV/2 and V/2 operated in the area of Oppeln which included the regions of Częstochowa, Radomsko, Piotrków Trybunalski, Końskie and Tomaszów Mazowiecki. In general the battalion was ordered to guard Polish army PoWs.

In the Łódź area Police Battalion I/3 was ordered to mop up the 'scattered remains of the Polish Army'. However, it also carried out numerous executions and repressive actions.

Around Poznań Police Battalion I/4 was instructed to round up Polish army stragglers that had not surrendered and carry out executions of any they deemed to be so-called 'plunderers, snipers and outlaws'.

Police Battalion I/5 operated in the north of the country and followed in the rear of the German 4th Army. It undertook a number of reconnaissance missions and probed the area for Polish army stragglers.

In the rear of the German 3rd Army was Police Battalion I/6 which was engaged in heavy fighting north-west of Warsaw in the areas of Grudziądz and Mława. It was formed in early September from a group of Berlin battalions, and its prime role during operations was to give protection to the rear of the 3rd Army as it moved southwards.

Also in the 3rd Army area of operations were the Police Battalions II/6 and III/6 which were engaged in operations north-west of Warsaw. They were also given orders to protect the rear of the advancing 3rd Army.

Along the northern coast in the newly-formed *Gau* (territory) of *Danzig-Westpreussen*, Police Battalion 1 that was formed in Berlin remained on alert in the city guarding administrative buildings in preparation for its capture by both Wehrmacht and *SS-Heimwehr Danzig* forces, the latter being an SS unit established in the Free City of Danzig.

Elsewhere, Police Battalion 2 was assigned duties north of Warsaw and assisted in the suppression of enemy forces including Jews when the Polish capital was captured.

Police Battalions 3 and 4 coincided with operations in the rear zone of the German 3rd Army. They were directly involved with the expulsion of Poles and Jews and chasing them across the Soviet border.

Police Battalion 5 was meanwhile operating and rounding up prisoners in the Kraków region, while Police Battalion 6 carried out a number of actions between 11 and 12 September, arresting some 900 Poles and executing a further 120 on the spot. Under the command of Hans Gabel who later joined the *Einsatzgruppe* D during fighting in Russia in 1941, a series of actions was ordered comprising the expulsion and shooting of Polish intelligentsia in the town of Bydgoszcz. Days later Gabel declared the town *judenfrei* ('free of Jews').

During the invasion of Poland German troops and Polish civilians stop on a bridge on the outskirts of Warsaw. Smoke can be seen rising from the capital following heavy ground and aerial bombardments.

Here Jews are seen lined up inside a Polish town and Order Policemen can be seen with them. During the invasion of Poland the SS-VT and *Einsatzgruppen* along with auxiliary personnel, SS and Order Police were tasked not with employing their military capabilities, but instead with terrorizing the civilian population through acts that included hunting down straggling Polish soldiers, confiscating livestock and agricultural produce and torturing and murdering large numbers of Polish political leaders, businessmen, priests, intellectuals and Jews.

Two photographs taken in sequence showing SS-VT (later *Waffen-SS*) soldiers and an Order Policeman checking the identification papers of a Jew on the streets of Kraków. Three SS-VT regiments had been deployed into the Polish heartlands consisting of *SS-Oberbayern*, *Brandenburg* and *Thüringen*. These soldiers in cooperation with the Order Police battalions quickly gained a reputation, and in a matter of days began eradicating the Poles by means of torture and killing those regarded as hostile to the Reich.

(**Above**) Order Policemen can be seen here escorting a bewildered Jewish gentleman along a street in Kraków. The Order Police battalions had been given a mission of 'cleansing and security measures' and their active duty in Poland would give the villages and towns through which they passed a fitting introduction to the character of Nazi rule.

(**Opposite, above**) An Order Police mock arrest of a comrade dressed up as a bearded Jewish pedlar by members of Police Battalion 101 in 1939. This battalion operated in Poland in late September in Łódź, Kielce, Lublin and along the border with the Soviet Union. *(United States Holocaust Memorial Museum – USHMM)*

(**Opposite, below**) Polish hostages in the Old Market Square in Bydgoszcz, Poland in September 1939 facing a wall in preparation for their execution. Roaming in the rear areas of the advancing SS-TV and Wehrmacht forces were the *Einsatzgruppen* and Order Police battalions. During their advance units roamed the countryside and as they came up to farmsteads and villages they wasted no time in conducting house searches, securing areas from insurgents and arresting and summarily shooting anyone they deemed to be 'suspicious elements' including Polish civilians and Jews. Similar atrocities included the torture and execution of political and religious leaders and even captured Polish soldiers. The mentally ill and the disabled including patients recuperating in hospitals or convalescing at home from various ailments or operations were murdered.

Order Police using their familiar tactic of rounding up suspected insurgents and getting them to crouch with their arms stretched out.

Polish women from the Pawiak and Mokotów prisons are led into the Palmiry forest for execution by SS-VT personnel supported by policemen. In a number of instances in Poland the Order Police assisted and participated in the large-scale killings of civilians and partisans. A number of police assisted the SS-VT regiments and participated in shooting prisoners of war and civilians, among them Jews.

The execution of Polish civilians by the *Selbstschutz* ethnic German self-defence organization, SS-VT and police in the forest near Tuchola-Bydgoszcz on 27 October 1939.

German soldiers rounding up a group of Jewish men on a street in Częstochowa. By the end of the Polish campaign it was estimated that some 531 towns and villages had been burned, during which the Wehrmacht supported by *Einsatzgruppen* and Order Police battalions carried out 714 mass executions along with many incidents of plunder, banditry and murder where they engaged in these killings on their own. Some 16,376 Poles fell victim to these acts of atrocities, the remainder of the murders being carried out by units of the *Einsatzgruppen*, SS-VT and Order Police.

Order Police support a Wehrmacht unit inside a Polish town rounding up Jews for a fate that can only be imagined. Although the Wehrmacht leadership in the main generally expressed disapproval relating to various acts of violence in the rear areas including the rounding up of Jews, they were in fact accomplices in these genocidal killings. The army leadership wanted to be kept out of the massacres as they deemed it damaging to the men's morale and discipline. Yet almost no one objected on principle and few opposed the orders or policies of committing war crimes.

The original caption reads: 'From a series of Nazi crimes during the occupation of Poland. The forest near Bochnia. Execution in the forest'. *(United States Holocaust Memorial Museum – USHMM, courtesy of Jacob Igra)*

An Order Police round-up of Jews in Tomaszów Mazowiecki. The Order Police involved in these actions were Police Battalion II/2. It was given duties such as rounding up Jews, soldiers who had not surrendered, collecting material abandoned by the Polish army and guarding captured prisoners. It also undertook a reprisal action against several hundred Polish people for the 'murder' of German soldiers.

Order Policemen were also tasked with the evacuation of Polish civilians and Jews from their homes. In this photograph Jewish people have been evicted from their homes and are more than likely being sent to a ghetto. The German government referred to these so-called ghettos as *Jüdischen Wohnbezirk* or *Wohngebiet der Juden*, both meaning Jewish Quarter. As soon as the German invasion of Poland had been achieved, plans were put into practice across the General Government region to create an extensive network of ghettos, while the rest of the country outside these isolated areas continued to endure harsh Nazi policies.

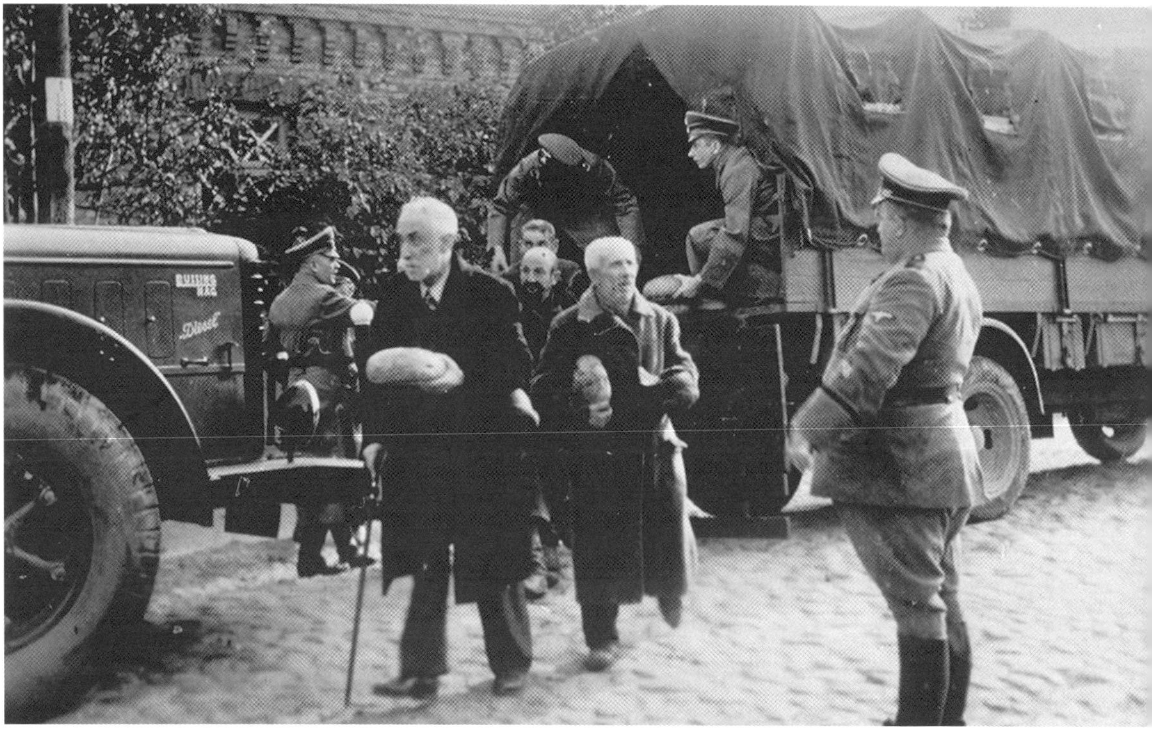

Here some old Jewish gentlemen have been given loaves of bread during an evacuation order. Such orders consisted of uprooting Polish Jews from their homes and businesses through compulsory expulsions. Entire Jewish communities were to be deported into special closed off zones by train from their places of origin using Order Police battalions. The police units were given strict orders to target the civilian population throughout the General Government area and were to carry out the expulsion of Poles from the *Reichsgau Wartheland* under the new *Lebensraum* policies.

Chief of the Order Police Kurt Daluege, NSKK official Adolf Hühnlein and police official Paul Riege review a parade at Kraków, probably in late 1939.

A Kattowitz sentry garrisoned at a District Order Police barracks in Poland in 1939. This man belongs to Police Battalion I/1. In Poland it was involved in the persecution of Jewish communities and against the so-called Polish intelligentsia.

Kurt Daluege greets Heinrich Himmler in the snow in Poland 1939 at a German police barracks in Kraków. Standing in the middle is Hans Frank, and Adjutant Becker can also be seen saluting.

German officers Daluege, Bodenschatz, Reichenau and Keitel in Poland, 13 September 1939.

Two photographs taken in sequence showing the rounding-up of fifty-two civilians from the city of Bochnia and its vicinity and the massacre that followed. The execution of the civilians which was committed by SS-TV troops and Order Policemen took place on 18 December 1939. This action was a reprisal for an attack on a German police officer two days earlier by the underground organization known as 'White Eagle'.

Two photographs taken in sequence showing joyful and festive policemen of Police Battalion 101 at Christmas 1940. During this period the battalion was tasked with surveillance of the Łódź Ghetto. They performed this task with regular local police.

The inspection of members of Police Battalion 101 by their Order Police officers in a public square in Łódź. *(United States Holocaust Memorial Museum – USHMM, courtesy of Michael O'Hara)*

Members of Police Battalion 101 are saluted by their Order Police officers as they march in formation in Łódź. *(United States Holocaust Memorial Museum – USHMM, courtesy of Michael O'Hara)*

Members of Police Battalion 101 during combat training in the vicinity of Łódź in 1940. In April and May the battalion returned to Germany where it underwent complete reorganization in Hamburg. The unit stayed in Germany for almost a year and was tasked with escorting three trainloads of Jews bound from Hamburg to the ghettos of Eastern Europe. It was later to return to Poland where it undertook genocide against Jews. *(United States Holocaust Memorial Museum – USHMM, courtesy of Michael O'Hara)*

Bernhardt Colberg, a member of Police Battalion 101, poses in front of their headquarters in the vicinity of Łódź. *(United States Holocaust Memorial Museum – USHMM, courtesy of Michael O'Hara)*

Members of Police Battalion 101 in their barracks in Łódź, 1940.
(United States Holocaust Memorial Museum – USHMM, courtesy of Michael O'Hara)

At an unidentified police station in Poland showing policemen in an office. Throughout 1940 and 1941 the Order Police were involved in the resettlement of millions of Jews into the General Government region. By the end of 1941 some 3.5 million Polish Jews had been segregated and ghettoized in a massive deportation action involving the use of hundreds of freight trains.

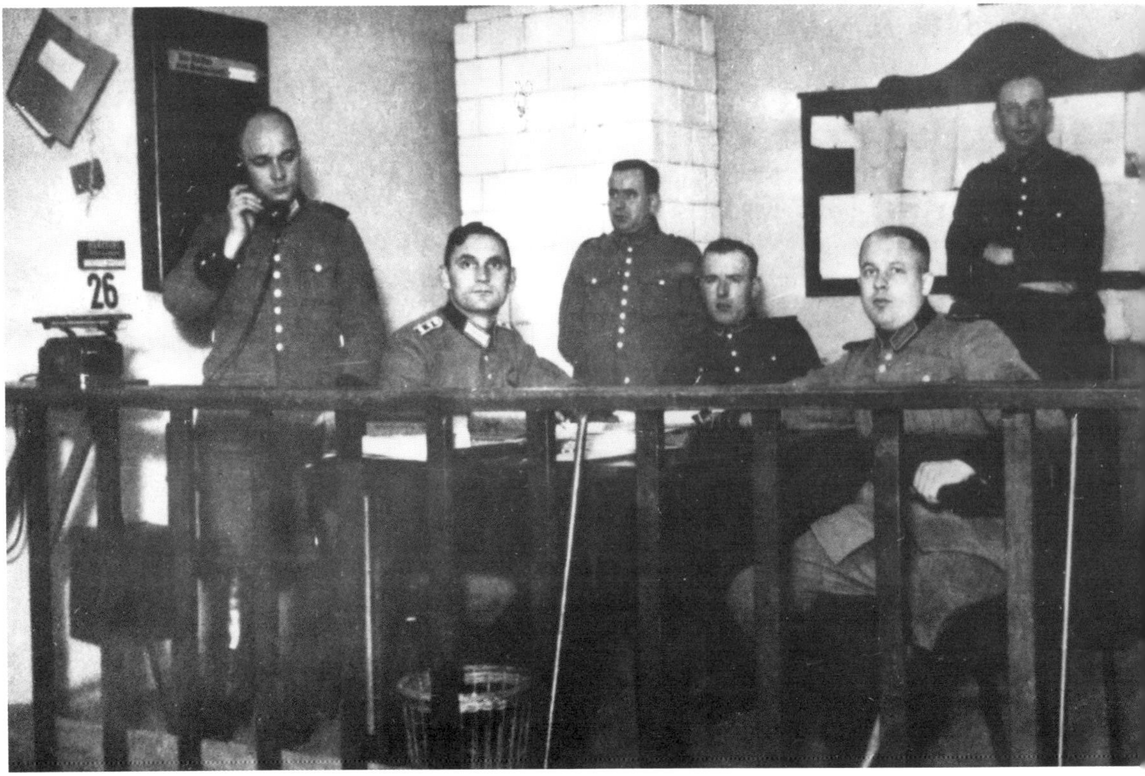

Chapter Three

Ghettos

(Transporting and Cleansing Actions)

Following the capture of Poland there was a period of more or less unrestrained terror. This included a series of operations comprising numerous police battalions assisting the *Einsatzgruppen* in a series of widespread cleansing actions across the country. In Pomerania alone, this period of terror continued with some 40,000 Poles including children being killed before the end of 1939.

The Nazis were determined to kill as many people as possible and prepare the Jews that still lived to be deported by railway to detention centres, concentration camps and ghettos. The Germans were going to make sure that Poland would be dismembered, subdivided and repopulated in such a way that it would never be able to rise against Germany again. What followed in Poland were plans drawn up facilitating the movement of vast numbers of people destined for what would initially be known as the General Government of the Occupied Polish Region. It consisted of the Polish province of Lublin and parts of the provinces of Warsaw and Kraków. Thousands of people would be more or less dumped in this region and were regarded by the Nazi government as enemies of the State.

Many of those who were resettled in the General Government area were frequently moved on foot and it was often the *Orpo* that were responsible for policing and escorting these huge numbers of people. They were also given a number of security tasks including traffic law enforcement and road safety administration. These were often controlled by motorized gendarmerie.

By February 1940 the immense problem of simultaneously attempting to relocate Poles and Jews had become such an administrative nightmare it was agreed that the Jews should be forced to live in ghettos. This would not only relieve the burden of the resettlement programme, it was also a way of temporarily halting the growing Jewish problem. After all, the Nazis hated and feared the Jews and to isolate them in ghettos was deemed immediately practicable. It was the General Government region consisting of a population of approximately 11 million people that was deemed the dumping ground for all undesirables and those regarded as enemies of the state. Thousands of Poles and Jews were deported into the General Government area where the first ghettos would be erected. The

Germans saw these ghettos purely as a provisional measure to control and segregate Jews while the Nazi leadership in Berlin deliberated on various means for their removal.

The Order Police would become an integral part of the resettlement programme of the Jews in Poland and join other German occupation forces in the Nazi persecution of the Jews and Poles. The so-called 'ghettoization action' of the Polish Jews across the General Government area was planned and headed by Hans Frank who was assigned Chief of Administration to the German military administration in occupied Poland. He became governor general of the occupied Polish territories. His main role was overseeing the General Government region and he assisted in and planned the segregation of the Jews and their 'ghettoization'. Frank's plan consisted of uprooting Polish Jews from their homes and businesses by implementing compulsory expulsions. Entire Jewish communities were to be deported into special zones closed off from their places of origin using a number of Order Police battalions. These battalions were given strict orders to target the civilian population throughout the General Government region and were to carry out the expulsion of Poles from the *Reichsgau Wartheland* under the new *Lebensraum* policies. They were told to use brutal measures in order to adhere to these policies and to commit whatever atrocities were required against the Jewish population as part of what they referred to as 'resettlement actions'.

Typically during the early part of the war there were two types of ghettos. The first was an open ghetto which did not have walls or fences, and the other was a closed or sealed ghetto which was often surrounded by brick walls, fences or barbed wire stretched between posts. Jews were not allowed to live in any other areas under the threat of punishment or even death. In order to prevent unauthorized contact between the Jewish and non-Jewish populations in the cities and towns, German Order Police battalions were assigned to patrol the perimeter of these new ghettos. Within each ghetto a Jewish Ghetto Police unit was formed to ensure that no prisoners tried to escape. One such battalion that was given the task of enforcing security measures was the Reserve Police Battalion 101. In the early summer of 1940 the battalion, comprising mainly regular policemen, was relocated to the Łódź area where it had been tasked with rounding up Poles who had escaped evacuation. It was later responsible for the 'surveillance of ghettos'. Its primary task as *Reserve-Polizei Bataillon Ghetto* was to patrol the perimeters of the Jewish ghettos, while internal security was undertaken by the SS, SD and the criminal police in conjunction with the Jewish ghetto administration. However, its tasks exceeded purely security measures, implementing both violence and shootings against those escorted to the ghettos and those already living there.

In April and May 1941 the battalion returned to Hamburg and underwent a complete reorganization. The men then carried out tasks supporting local police units in escorting trainloads of Jews from Hamburg who were bound for ghettos across Eastern Europe. In a report dated 24 October 1941, during these escort operations there were 16 *Ordnungspolizei* men escorting the trains for every 1,000 Jews deported.

In June 1942 Police Battalion 101 consisting of 11 officers and 491 men of various ranks returned to Poland where it was involved in a number of massacres and various killings. It was given security duties in which it was actively escorting Jews during 'ghetto cleansing actions' in which it supported the SS during what was known as *Aktion Reinhardt*. This action meant the liquidation of the ghettos across the General Government area and sending Jews to three Reinhardt camps specifically constructed for murder, which were Treblinka, Sobibor and Belzec. The police battalion, together with members of the Jewish police, the *Sonderdienst* battalion of Ukrainian Trawnikis supported by regular SS soldiers, was ordered to march into the ghettos and immediately begin rounding up the Jews to liquidate the ghettos. This liquidation process meant the Jews being either marched out of the ghetto or loaded onto waiting trucks and transported either directly to the camps or on board railway cattle or freight cars to their destination.

The liquidation of the camps was often undertaken barbarically. Regularly policemen would beat and whip Jews in the streets. They would then be forced out of the ghetto and transported to their fate, often to the 'Reinhardt Camps'. The Częstochowa Ghetto, for instance, saw the majority of its 40,000 inhabitants removed onto trains under the guise of resettlement, sent directly to the Treblinka death camp and murdered. Others such as the Międzyrzec Ghetto would see some 11,000 to 12,000 Jews rounded up by German Order Police battalions and deported to Treblinka. In the Minsk Ghetto some 5,000 Jews were forced out of their squalid living conditions and onto freight trains bound for Treblinka.

During a number of the ghetto cleansing actions policemen were told not to transport the Jews to the death camps but to systematically murder them instead. Thousands of people were killed in this way. Around 4,500 Jews from the Izbica Ghetto were marched out of the place on foot and killed before being disposed of in mass pits by police battalions and the SS. The Lida Ghetto saw almost 6,000 Jews forced out and taken to a nearby military firing range where they were shot into grave pits. In the summer of 1942, the Nowogródek Ghetto was liquidated and this began by murdering members of the *Judenrat* (Jewish council) who were either shot or hung. This was followed by about 1,200 Jews being forced out of the town and marched to the Kurpiesze Forest where they were all shot so they fell into hastily prepared pits. On 6 August 1942, the final part of the liquidation of the ghetto took place with another massacre. Some 2,000 to 3,000 Jews were executed into mass graves in the Jewish cemetery on the southern outskirts of Zdzięcioł.

Across many of the ghettos the liquidation process was undertaken in phases so that the removal of the Jews could be completed effectively by the German authorities. At the Końskowola Ghetto the majority of the inhabitants were rounded up in the summer of 1942 and transported to the Sobibor extermination camp. It was not until October 1942 that the ghetto population would be entirely liquidated. However, the remaining Jews would not be transported to their death. Instead the Reserve Police Battalion 101 carried out a massacre of some 800 to 1,000 Jews, among them women and children. The frightened inhabitants were taken to a nearby forest and murdered. The ghetto's remaining Jews were transferred to another camp. At the Buczacz Ghetto in the summer of 1942 some 4,500 Jews were either murdered or transported to the Belzec death camp.

By mid-1943 the liquidation of the ghettos in the General Government region was almost complete, and the death camps were receiving many of the last deliveries by early summer. The police battalions had played a key part in the implementation of escorting the Jewish people to their deaths. They had indiscriminately murdered men, women and children during these cleansing actions. Those that were not sent to the various labour camps or death factories were murdered during mass executions at secluded killing sites. By the end of the war some 3 million Jews had died in occupied Poland at the hands of the Nazis. The establishment of the ghettos of Poland had played a pivotal part in the Holocaust. The police battalions had also been absolutely complicit in the Nazi success of cleansing most of the ghettos and sending many innocent men, women and children to their deaths.

Local police auxiliaries and Order Police assist in the evacuation and removal of Jews by *Güterwagen* (freight wagons) either to ghettos or to concentration camps.

Here Jews are being transported by ferry across the Vistula River for resettlement in the Kraków Ghetto. It was in March 1941 that the establishment of this ghetto was ordered, and it was founded in the Podgórze district of Kraków in April 1941 and was soon enclosed by a wall of barbed wire and stone.

A photograph showing the evacuation of men, women and children being escorted by local police auxiliaries and Order Police through a town. The police units were given strict orders to target the civilian population throughout the General Government region and were to carry out the expulsion of Poles from the *Reichsgau Wartheland* under the new *Lebensraum* policies. Poles were often resettled and Jews were either sent to ghettos or murdered.

An Order Policeman with an upset Jewish boy during a settlement action into a ghetto.

Jews moving their belongings under police supervision into the Grodno Ghetto which was erected in November 1941. The ghetto was divided into two areas, one in the old part of the city around the synagogue. Some 15,000 Jews were forced to live in this area. The other ghetto was established in the Slobodka suburb with some 10,000 Jews living in this district.

(United States Holocaust Memorial Museum – USHMM, courtesy of Jacob Igra)

Jewish deportees carrying their bundles and suitcases march through town towards the railway station behind Nazi officials riding in an open car.

Local police supported by Order Police loading Jewish people aboard a train during an evacuation order to a ghetto. It was agreed to move large numbers of Jews to the ghettos, especially if they were some distance from their dwellings, the *Deutsche Reichsbahn* (German National Railway) would be used along with the Polish National Railways (PKP) which had been handed over to the Germans to operate.

Two photographs taken in sequence of Order Policemen during the liquidation of the Lublin Ghetto.

German police standing in formation in Zawiercie. Some 7,000 Jews lived in this town and in the summer of 1940 a formal ghetto was established. That autumn about 500 young Jews were deported to labour camps in Germany. The ghetto was liquidated on 26 August 1943 when most of the remaining Jews were deported to Auschwitz. During the deportation action 100 Jews were murdered by police units.

Order Police checking Jews at a market in Lublin. The Lublin Ghetto was erected in March 1941 and mainly housed Polish Jews, but there were also some transports of Roma inhabitants. Between mid-March and mid-April 1942 during the ghetto's liquidation more than 30,000 Jews were sent to Belzec and an additional 4,000 to Majdanek where they were subsequently murdered.

The bundles and suitcases of the Jewish deportees are loaded onto a moving van. The Jews of Würzburg and such other Mainfranken communities as Aschaffenburg, Schweinfurt, Kitzingen and Bad Kissingen were rounded up and deported to ghettos and concentration camps in the East in a series of transports beginning in early November 1941. Order Policemen often humiliated the Jews during the deportation process which also included the confiscation of many of their personal belongings.

Members of Police Battalion 101 beneath a sign that reads 'Krzewie'.
(United States Holocaust Memorial Museum – USHMM, courtesy of Michael O'Hara)

A night-time view of members of Police Battalion 101 guarding the perimeter of the Łódź Ghetto. Between June 1942 and November 1943 the battalion was assigned to support the liquidation of the ghetto, which consisted of not only assisting in their transportation to the extermination camps but also murdering them through mass shootings. They were also ordered to remove the Jews, with the aid of Trawnikis, from the Lublin, Izbica, Zamość, Kraśnik, Łomazy, Parczew, Międzyrzec, Radzyń, Łuków, Końskowola, Tomaszow, Serokomla and Kock ghettos.
(United States Holocaust Memorial Museum – USHMM, courtesy of Michael O'Hara)

A member of Police Battalion 101 [probably Bernhardt Colberg] poses at the entrance of Guard Post 5 in the Łódź Ghetto in 1941. It was here that Battalion 101 was given duties of policing and guarding the ghetto. *(United States Holocaust Memorial Museum – USHMM, courtesy of Michael O'Hara)*

A member of Police Battalion 101 poses here next to a large sign marking the entrance to the Łódź Ghetto in 1940. *(United States Holocaust Memorial Museum – USHMM, courtesy of Michael O'Hara)*

Two members of Police Battalion 101 who are guarding the perimeter of the Łódź Ghetto view three Jewish policemen kneeling opposite them on the other side of the fence.
(United States Holocaust Memorial Museum – USHMM, courtesy of Michael O'Hara)

Łódź residents line up at an unidentified office in the ghetto. Some 160,000 Jews from the city were crammed into the ghetto and the area was isolated from the rest of Łódź with barbed-wire fencing. The ghetto was divided into three sections by the intersection of two major roads. By January 1942, with the assistance of the Order Police, the first stages of the liquidation of the ghetto began with 70,000 Jews being deported to the Chełmno killing centre. Following the first part of its liquidation there were no more deportations until May 1944 when some 3,000 Jews were sent to Chełmno. Three months later the final part of the liquidation of the ghetto was untaken with the surviving residents being sent to Auschwitz-Birkenau.

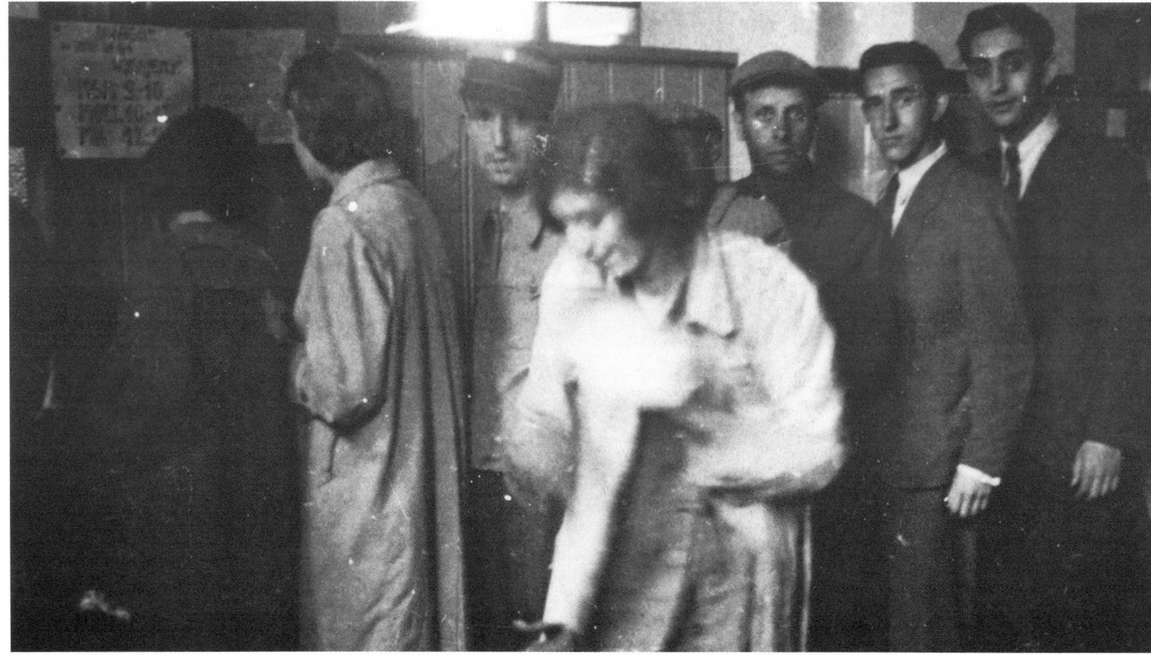

Ghetto police guard a group of Jewish men who have been lined up in the yard of the central prison of the Łódź Ghetto.

Jewish police guard a group of central European Jews who have been assembled for deportation in the central prison of the Łódź Ghetto.

A German official supervises a deportation action in the Kraków Ghetto. Jews assembled in a courtyard with their bundles are awaiting further instructions. When the ghetto was initially erected it was populated by approximately 16,000 Jews. The site was divided into two parts: Ghetto 'A' and Ghetto 'B'. Ghetto 'A' was intended for the work force and Ghetto 'B' for the remaining Jews who were incarcerated. This division was purely for ease and segregation for the liquidation of the ghetto, which began in stages from 30 May 1942 onwards. The Order Police together with local police units and *Waffen-SS* began systematically deporting Jews to surrounding concentration camps. The first transport consisted of 7,000 and the second 4,000 Jews, all of whom were deported to the Belzec death camp on 5 June 1942. However, the final liquidation of the ghetto was not carried out until 13–14 March 1943.

An Order Policeman checks the identification papers of Jews in the Kraków Ghetto.

Order Police load Jews onto trucks in the Ciechanów Ghetto during a liquidation action.

A street scene with Jewish police in the Będzin Ghetto which was created in the town in July 1940. Some 20,000 local Jews from Będzin along with an additional 10,000 Jews removed from neighbouring areas by the Order Police were forced into the ghetto. All able-bodied people were forced to work in German military factories before the ghetto was finally liquidated and the Jews that had not died of disease, hunger or mistreatment were transported by train to the nearby concentration camp at Auschwitz where they were exterminated. The last major deportation of the ghetto saw an uprising between 1 and 3 August 1943 which was marked by members of the Jewish Combat Organization.

(**Above**) An Order Policeman checks the papers of a Jewish cyclist on a street in the Warsaw Ghetto, which was the largest of all the Jewish ghettos, not only in Poland but in all of occupied Europe. It was established in November 1940, and at its peak as many as 460,000 Jews were held there within its brick walls. It was not until the summer of 1942 when the first part of the ghetto was liquidated by local police, Order Police and *Waffen-SS* units. This consisted of a massive deportation action with some 265,000 ghetto residents being sent to the newly-opened Treblinka extermination camp and another 20,000 being sent to labour camps. This process took some eight to twelve weeks to achieve.

(**Opposite**) A member of the Jewish ghetto police stands outside a house in the Kovno Ghetto. Due to the fact that the Order Police and local police units were often overstretched with guarding numerous ghettos, Jewish men were initially recruited as policemen with white armbands to maintain order and discipline in the ghettos and enforce the orders of the Jewish council.

(**Above**) Order Police can be seen here inside a vehicle at the entrance to a ghetto.

(**Opposite, above**) Order Police supporting Wehrmacht troops can be seen here assisting Jewish women and children into freight cars bound for a concentration camp. The Order Police often rounded up and transported the Jews to the trains while local auxiliaries or collaborators supported the operation. Those coordinating the transportation were told to lie to the Jews about their intentions by portraying their train journeys as a 'resettlement in the East'. However, in reality the 'resettlement in the East' was just a ploy for transportation to either the concentration camps or the new death camps.

(**Opposite, below**) Order Police are seen here escorting Jewish people with their belongings destined for a concentration camp. Once a communiqué had been sent through the appropriate channels of the SS, local auxiliaries including members of the Order Police were ordered to assist the transports. The police were told to escort the Jews with an element of calm in order to ensure there was no initial panic. Deception and disguise were key to the whole operation.

A policeman can be seen here standing at a railway siding. During 1942 all across Poland and other parts of occupied Europe trains were transporting deportees directly to the concentration camps. However, there were numerous camps that did not have railway platforms. Often those who arrived had to walk miles to reach their destination.

The liquidation of a Polish ghetto in 1942 by an Order Police battalion. The Germans had announced the launch of 'a resettlement in the East'. However, in reality these evacuations of the ghettos were to transport Jews directly to concentration camps and eradicate most of them through extreme hard labour or death in the gas chambers.

Chapter Four

Russia 1941–42

When the Nazi war machine launched its attack against the Soviet Union on 22 June 1941, the Jewish crisis escalated further. To deal with these problems as the Wehrmacht and *Waffen-SS* advanced through the Baltic States battling their way against withdrawing Red Army forces, four *Einsatzgruppen* were used in the rear areas. These units were divided into A, B, C and D and were under the operational control of the higher SS police chiefs in its zone of operations. The first three groups were attached to Army Group North, Centre and South, while D was assigned to the 11th Army in the Crimea. Their missions were 'cleansing and security measures', and their active duty in the East would give the villages and towns through which they passed a fitting introduction to the character of Nazi rule.

As for a number of the Order Police battalions, they were ordered into Russia to operate both independently and in conjunction with the *Einsatzgruppen*. On 11 June 1941 an instruction of the OKH ordered the use of police units joined to security divisions. Although it outlined that the police would be assigned to anti-partisan tasks as well as escorting PoWs, it was also to play a more sinister role in operations as it had done in Poland. This included terrorizing the civilian population through acts that included hunting down straggling Russian soldiers, confiscating livestock and agricultural produce, and torturing and murdering large numbers of Polish political leaders, businessmen, priests, intellectuals and Jews. Just prior to the invasion the police units were told that the war in Russia would be no normal war, it was an 'ideological war of extermination'. In the eyes of the Nazis the Soviet Union represented the home of Bolshevism and international Jewry which needed to be both rooted out and destroyed.

Numerous police battalions were transported to the East to undertake various types of what were deemed 'security measures'. Police Battalion 105 was sent to the Baltic States and carried out rear cleansing operations in Latvia with the *Einsatzgruppen*. It then advanced into Estonia where it entered Russian territory following the fighting Wehrmacht units. Here it remained at Gdov on the eastern shore of Lake Peipus for approximately three weeks. It then carried out a number of anti-partisan operations, hanging and killing Russians. Later in the year as the Russian lines stiffened and fighting intensified, the battalion was embroiled in combat and suffered severe losses. As the military situation remained precarious throughout the winter and into spring, the battalion continued fighting in the Ljuban region.

Another Police Battalion to operate in the Baltic States was No. 321. It was transferred to Kaunas in Lithuania where it undertook 'pacification actions' along with the *Einsatzgruppen* in June and early July 1941. These actions dealt with local criminals released from prison along with nationalistic and anti-Semitic groups. Some 4,000 Jews were killed either on the streets of the city or escorted to nearby open pits and ditches and massacred. Following the Kaunas pogrom the battalion then advanced across the Baltics where it entered Russian territory. It was here in the Soviet Union that the battalion undertook numerous security operations, but due to heavy fighting was compelled to support the *SS-Totenkopf* Division close to the city of Demjansk. It later became trapped within a large Russian pocket with the entire II Army Corps from 8 February to April 1942.

In May of that year Police Battalion 111 was sent to central Russia where it was ordered to undertake security tasks and also supporting actions carried out by the Security Police (*Sicherheitspolizei* or *SiPo*). It was in the area of Vitebsk that the battalion along with security police units carried out a number of killing actions against Russian partisans.

During the same period Police Battalion 112 was sent to northern Russia from the Netherlands where it operated in the rear area of the German 18th Army from June 1942. Also transported to northern Russia was Police Battalion 121. It was airlifted from Vichy France in January 1942 where it fought directly in the Leningrad area. The battalion was later disbanded in the summer where it joined the *SS-Polizei* Division around Kolpino. This division had been formed back in October 1939 when thousands of members of the Order Police were drafted to fill the ranks of the new SS division. At that time these men were not actually enrolled in the SS but technically remained policemen, retaining their police rank structure and insignia.

Other police battalions also operated in Russia including No. 122 where it conducted anti-partisan activities in the spring and summer of 1942. Police Battalion 131 on the other hand was instructed to accompany the *Einsatzgruppen* near Suwałki where it acted as a reserve battalion. It was directly involved in the murder of Jews in Belorussia in June and July 1941.

Across the Eastern provinces of the Soviet Union the police battalions that operated alongside the *Einsatzgruppen* swept across large areas, roaming and searching as they advanced, killing as many Soviet and Jewish communities as possible. Assisting in these massacres the Order Police had the help of local police units and auxiliaries. Many of the killings, especially in the Ukraine and Belorussia, were undertaken by fellow Ukrainians and Belarusians commanded by German officers.

Numerous police battalions were involved in massacres including No. 133 which participated in the killing of Jews and partisans at Kołomyja, Deliatin, Jaremcze and Drohobycz. Between October 1941 and the summer of 1942 it is estimated that some 15,000 victims were killed by this particular battalion alone. In addition it also escorted some 8,000 deportees to their death at the Belzec concentration camp.

Other battalions also conducted a number of brutal massacres. Police Battalion 303 was one of six that operated in the Ukraine during the initial stages of the invasion of the Soviet Union. It was not only engaged in mopping up Soviet pockets of resistance, but also undertook security actions against the local population which included hanging partisans and razing farmsteads to the ground. It was also involved in the massacre at Chudniv in early September 1941, killing hundreds of Jews, and it operated alongside *Einsatzkommando* squads in actions where many people were slaughtered in and around Zhitomir. The thoroughness and brutality with which these 'cleansing actions' were conducted were both violent and ruthless. Police Battalion 303 along with the *Einsatzgruppen* undertook a number of actions in the rear areas targeting the Jewish population, and Babi Yar was one of the most brutal massacres of the war involving Police Battalion 303. Between 29 and 30 September 1941 more than 33,000 Jews were murdered at Babi Yar, and over the following months this place remained in use as an execution site for gypsies and Soviet prisoners of war.

The murders did not end at Babi Yar either as the police battalions went on to hunt down partisans and Soviet army stragglers. Their killing spree was only halted by the onset of winter in the rear of Army Group South. A number of policemen were actually decorated for their 'pacification activities' and were awarded with medals for their so-called 'valour'.

During 1942 more police battalions were given 'special tasks' on the Eastern Front involving a variety of duties, mainly killing actions and mopping up the rear areas. However, there were units like Police Battalion 305 which was sent to the Leningrad Front where it became part of a front-line infantry division. Its main task was to reinforce I Army Corps in the area of Puschkino-Krasnoye Selo and was titled *Polizei-Kampfgruppe Jeckeln*.

Other police battalions including No. 324 were also sent to the Leningrad Front to support the *Polizei* Division fighting along the front lines. In fact the personnel were re-equipped with divisional uniforms. However, its existence as a battalion in Russia was short-lived and it was disbanded in the autumn of 1941.

Numerous other police battalions were sent to Russia for the purpose of so-called 'police duties' or as army reinforcements. Police Battalion 306 was sent to the Soviet Union on the Leningrad Front. It had already been involved in various heinous actions in Poland where it carried out shootings of Jews along with Police Battalion 307 in the area of Biała Podlaska and the murder of former Polish officers. It had also been given tasks such as evacuations and arrests and was ordered to shoot Polish peasants who were late with paying their rural taxes. Now in Russia Police Battalion 306 was assigned as 'army reinforcement'. As for Police Battalion 307, it continued its action in the Brest-Litovsk region where the whole battalion perpetrated mass genocide. It also supported operations alongside *Einsatzkommando* 8.

As fighting intensified in the heartlands of the Soviet Union, more and more land was conquered by German Wehrmacht and *Waffen-SS* formations. As a result there were massive Red Army surrenders. Consequently this caused logistical and organizational difficulties for the German authorities with containing the PoWs. Various PoW camps were erected and the prisoners who did not starve to death were often sent to labour or concentration camps across the Nazi domain. Police Battalion 308 along with many other police units was ordered to escort thousands of Soviet PoWs and carry out mass executions. Already this battalion had been involved in a number of genocide actions. It included suppression around the Warsaw Ghetto which included reprisals against Poles and Jews. It also acted as the main armed escort for the death trains destined for the concentration and extermination camps of Auschwitz, Buchenwald and Ravensbrück.

Though the systematic murder of Russian PoWs was regarded as a necessity to relieve the growing burden of containing the soldiers in camps, Himmler wanted many hundreds of thousands transported to labour camps to work them to death for the German war effort. As a result, numerous police battalions escorted the PoWs to trains destined for labour or concentration camps.

Another problem encountered by the German authorities in Russia was the growing number of partisans. Even as early as in the summer of 1941 this became a major concern. As a result police battalions were given the task of road security in order to safeguard major motorways which were ordered to be kept open for military traffic advancing eastwards. Police Battalion 309 was one of many police units assigned to road security. It followed the advance of the 2nd Panzer Army towards Orel during its advance on Moscow. In the village of Yefremov it was involved in a partisan action. The battalion continued with road security duties and partisan actions until May 1942.

Other security measures to combat partisan attacks were also implemented including railway protection. Police Battalion 310 was given the task of both road and rail security. It had operated in Poland in 1940 and had already murdered alleged Polish partisans. It was then transferred to Galicia in early August 1941 where for the next six months it was assigned to guard duties, civil protection, road security, anti-airborne patrols, air-raid protection and anti-smuggling black market operations, the mopping-up of Russian stragglers, armed escorts of freight transports, escorting and shootings of Soviet PoWs and raids in the Lwów (modern-day Lviv) Ghetto which included seizures and arrests.

Police Battalion 311 also operated in and around Lwów where it took part in mopping-up actions and the execution of a number of Jews. However, the battalion was officially responsible for anti-partisan operations. Another police unit responsible for anti-partisan actions was Police Battalion 316. It was also ordered to mop up Soviet stragglers and execute them. Its successful mopping-up actions earned the respect of many of its commanders and some policemen were actually awarded with medals and other decorations. The battalion then went on to operate in the urban area of Mogilev where it was responsible along with Police Battalion 322 for the murders in the local Jewish ghetto. Later in 1941 it was given road security duties along the motorway between Orsha and Smolensk.

Also operating in the region of Orsha was Police Battalion 317 which took part in both security and anti-partisan actions and was flanked by Police Battalions 309 and 131. Once again the policemen were awarded decorations for their operations which had included the murdering of Jews blamed for allegedly assisting partisan actions against the German authorities. The police battalions were also assigned to the Wehrmacht security divisions until July 1942.

While security actions continued mercilessly, other police battalions carried on with various cleansing actions comprising numerous mass executions. Police Battalion 318 was involved in the execution of Jews and communists in the latter part of 1941. By the summer of 1942 it was relocated east of the Dnieper River where it undertook a 'pacification drive against bandits and paratroopers in a wooded area south of Nowoja-Bassan' which was launched on 4 and 5 July. Also operating in the Ukraine was Police Battalion 319. Although its cleansing actions were undertaken on a comparatively smaller scale than Police Battalion 318, its operations in the heartlands of the Ukraine were deemed effective and pacification was successful.

One police unit, however, which was responsible for the murders of around 45,000 people, was Police Battalion 320. It crossed over the Soviet border in the middle of August 1941 and its advance eastwards led it to the towns and cities of Przemyśl, Lwów and Tarnopol. Its mission was for 'special employment' and from the moment it was employed the battalion would regularly be involved in genocide actions against the Jewish communities. The police units undertook a series of widespread massacres in Stara Konstantinova, Kamianets Podilskyi, Minkovsky, Zwianczyk and Sokolek. Those that managed to escape the slaughter were hunted down and killed. The police battalion was later given anti-partisan duties in February 1942 and then transferred south along the Mius River in the area of Taganrog at the rear of the 1st Panzer Army.

Another police battalion given anti-partisan operations was No. 322. When it advanced through Russian territory in June 1941 it undertook road block duties, patrols and house searches in and around the city of Bialystok. It was also given orders for the 'drastic reduction of the Jewish community' in Bialystok in the nearby forest of Pietrasze. Following the slaughter of some 5,000 Jews in the forest the battalion was transferred to Białowieża to undertake an evacuation order of a large forested area that *Reichsmarschall* Hermann Göring wanted for his hunting lodge. The entire local population was dispatched to other areas. The battalion was then transferred to Minsk where it was assigned to carry out an action against the ghetto. The Jews were driven out of their squalid living conditions and a number of them were murdered in the process. In October the battalion was ordered to brutally 'clean out' the Mogilev Ghetto.

Alongside Police Battalion 322 was Police Battalion 323 which operated initially in the region of Bialystok. Its main task, however, was 'pacification/resettlement actions' which involved driving out the local population from several villages and hamlets between July and October 1941. It was also involved in guarding the Bialystok Ghetto and mopping-up operations from July 1941 to May 1942.

By summer 1942, across the Eastern provinces of the Soviet Union both the Wehrmacht and *Waffen-SS* had swept across large areas. Behind them *Einsatzgruppen*, police battalions, auxiliaries and local police had roamed the countryside, searching as they advanced and killing off as many Soviet and Jewish communities as possible. Many of the killings, especially in the Ukraine and Belorussia, were undertaken by fellow Ukrainians and Belarusians commanded by German officers. Yet despite the successful operations, the massacres were reduced until the widespread liquidation of the ghettos began across Europe and the Eastern territories.

By the summer of 1942, as further military events prevented the German war machine from winning the war on the Eastern Front, many of the police battalions were disbanded and re-consolidated into the *Waffen-SS* divisions or the SS police regiments. Between 1942 and 1943 there were thirty SS police regiments formed from the existing Order Police. Many of these regiments were created for security duties in occupied Europe.

(**Opposite**) This propaganda postcard shows two policemen standing guard at the front. 'German Police Day', symbolizing the comradeship and unity between the Order Police and the *Waffen-SS* on the front line in the East. The Nazis went to great lengths to symbolically link the Order Police to the regime. In various publications and public events the police were depicted as an important part of the Nazi organization and the protectors of the so-called 'national community'. These events included dedication ceremonies, commemorations and festivities such as the 'Day of the German Police', which built on Weimar-era traditions of festivals meant to improve public opinion of the police.

(**Below**) Order Police and Wehrmacht troops entering a Russian town in preparation for a cleansing action. When German forces attacked the Soviet Union on 22 June 1941, the Jewish problem escalated. For the Nazi empire the prospect of a war against Russia entailed a transition from one policy of murder to another. As Hitler had explained to his generals just a few months prior to the invasion, this war would be no normal war; it would be an 'ideological war of extermination'. The Order Police were ordered to advance in the rear areas of the German forces and undertake what were termed 'cleansing actions'.

DIE
POLIZEI
IM FRONTEINSATZ
TAG DER DEUTSCHEN POLIZEI

Local residents watch as the Germans publicly hang a woman on a gallows erected in the town square by Police Battalion 101. *(United States Holocaust Memorial Museum – USHMM)*

German police hanging a man in a village, someone most likely suspected of being a partisan. The police battalions undertook widespread anti-partisan operations in Russia including hanging and killing Russian partisans. *(United States Holocaust Memorial Museum – USHMM)*

(**Above**) The bodies of two men hanging from a gallows following a public execution by Order Police Battalion 101. Across the whole zone of operations units conducted mass shootings and engaged in public hangings which were used as a terror tactic on the local population.
(United States Holocaust Memorial Museum – USHMM)

(**Opposite, above**) An Order Police line-up prior to an operation. The Order Police were one of the two primary units from which the *Einsatzgruppen* drew personnel with regard to their requirements in the rear areas along with the *Waffen-SS*.

(**Opposite, below**) Order Police during a massacre in the rear area of the Soviet Union. Order Police battalions involved in direct killing operations were responsible for at least 1 million murders.

An Order Police battalion on parade with their commanding officer. For operations in the rear area of Russia there were two battalions assigned to support the *Einsatzgruppen* which carried out widespread massacres against Soviet PoWs, partisans, Jews and anyone regarded as hostile to the Nazis.

Order Policemen relaxing while billeted in a Ukrainian town during operations in 1941. The police played a vital role in the execution of the Holocaust in the Ukraine and supported the extensively widespread executions of Jewish communities.

Order Police officers posing for the camera during operations in the Ukraine in 1941. There were six police battalions that operated in the Ukraine during the initial stages of the invasion of the Soviet Union. They were not only engaged in mopping up Soviet pockets of resistance, but also undertaking security actions against the local population including hanging partisans and razing farmsteads to the ground.

Police officers touring the rear areas during operations in the Ukraine in 1941.

Police officers and Wehrmacht officers can be seen here touring the rear areas of conquered territory in the Ukraine in the summer of 1941. The police battalions were subordinate to the SS and not under the command of the German army. Their primary role in the Soviet Union was deployment in areas of German-occupied Europe while operating in the rear areas of the Wehrmacht, *Waffen-SS* and *Einsatzgruppen* in Russia.

Two photographs showing police and Wehrmacht officers at a garrison set up in the Ukraine during the summer of 1941.

During a massacre of suspected partisans an Order Police unit can be seen here with their rifles as part of a firing squad.

German police and auxiliaries in civilian clothes look on as a group of Jewish women are forced to undress before their execution. This photograph is part of a group of images showing members of the community from the Mizocz Ghetto undressing before their massacre. This ghetto had initially held some 1,700 Jews. On 13 October 1942, the eve of the ghetto's liquidation, some of the inhabitants rose up against the Germans and were defeated after a short battle. The remaining members of the community were transported from the ghetto to a ravine in Zdolbuniv, south of Rovno. At the edge of the ravine the Jews, mostly women and children, were ordered to undress and then were herded down the ravine and executed. *(United States Holocaust Memorial Museum – USHMM Instytut Pamięci Narodowej)*

A German policeman is seen here shooting the remaining inhabitants of the Mizocz Ghetto that were still showing signs of life. Note the young child still sitting upright, obviously terrified by the whole spectacle. *(United States Holocaust Memorial Museum – USHMM Instytut Pamięci Narodowej)*

Assisting the Order Police were also local police units and auxiliaries pictured here. Many of the killings, especially in the Ukraine and Belorussia, were undertaken by fellow Ukrainians and Belarusians commanded by German officers.

(**Above**) Police officers escort female Soviet civilians away during a partisan operation in September 1942. Anyone arrested and suspected of partisan activity was either shot or hanged.

(**Opposite, above**) Order Policemen supported by Hungarian personnel can be seen here rounding up terrified local inhabitants of the town of Chernigov in the Ukraine in 1942. During this so-called reprisal action the police and Hungarians almost totally burned the town to the ground and the population that lived there was exterminated. Some 6,700 people were murdered and 1,290 homes burned. The destruction of this town together with its inhabitants was the largest single 'reprisal raid' of the Nazi occupation in the Ukraine during the war. *(Hungarian National Museum)*

(**Below**) *SS-Reichsführer* Heinrich Himmler accepting the good wishes of SS, police officers and SS policemen on the occasion of his birthday at SS headquarters in the Hegewald bei Zhitomir compound in the Ukraine.

Chapter Five

Other Areas of Operations 1939–42

While the police battalions were heavily established across the Reich and supporting Wehrmacht, *Waffen-SS* and *Einsatzgruppen* forces in the Baltics and the Soviet Union, they were also located in occupied countries including lands that were annexed by the Nazis. In fact the Order Police participated in the annexation of Austria and the occupation of the Sudetenland in 1938. By 1939 there were almost 100,000 Order Police. There was also a large police presence in the Protectorate of Bohemia and Moravia. These Czech lands were partially annexed territory of Nazi Germany which was established in March 1939. The protectorate was in principle an independent state, but had a dual system of government. German laws applied to ethnic Germans, while other residents had the legal status of the Protectorate and were governed by a puppet Czech administration.

Across the Protectorate police battalions were often named according to the district in which they were stationed. In the Czech capital Prague was the so-called Police Battalion *Prague*. It became operational in the city in October 1939, but was transferred to Poland in December of that year. By the summer of 1941 part of the battalion was transferred to Russia, while the remaining companies operated in Prague. On 10 June 1942 it was involved in the reprisal action at Lidice following the assassination of *Reichsprotektor* Reinhard Heydrich. The reprisal action saw the complete destruction of the village, the execution of 173 male inhabitants and the deportation of the women to Ravensbrück and the children to Łódź.

In the weeks following the death of Heydrich the Order Police began a repressive wave of measures by taking aggressive action against the inhabitants of Prague. Many companies were mobilized from numerous police administrations of the Reich and sent to Bohemia and Moravia. This action was known as a 'mopping-up' operation and involved some 2,630 policemen and 84 officers across the towns and cities of Dresden, Vienna, Breslau, Berlin, Potsdam, Troppau, Waldenburg, Würzburg and Leipzig which were assigned to the local garrisons of Brunn, Iglau, Holleschau and Mährisch-Ostrau. In total there were twenty-two companies mobilized following Heydrich's assassination. Each police company was told to enforce German rule over the Protectorate and implement a free reign of terror for the bloody reprisal of the death of the *Reichsprotektor*. Immediately following the attack on Heydrich martial law was enforced, causing widespread arrests with people being rounded up by the police and sent to the Gestapo headquarters in Prague where they were tortured and killed. Thousands of people were also sent to concentration camps. In the days immediately following the attack there were 247 death sentences passed by the SS.

For the Czech population of the Protectorate of Bohemia and Moravia there was an increased period of oppression. Police units were ordered to search houses, randomly set up road blocks and undertake surveillance on suspected anti-Nazis or those classified by the German authorities as enemies of the Reich. These were chiefly people believed to be involved in the resistance movement, communists and the Jewish community.

During 1941 there were more than 90,000 Jews living in Bohemia and Moravia, the majority of whom would be sent to the concentration camps. A number of police units were responsible for escorting the Jews to transit stations where they were loaded onto overcrowded freight cars and sent further east.

South-west of Prague in the district of Pilzen and Klattau Jewish communities were also being persecuted and publically humiliated by the Order Police. Police Battalion *Klattau* operated in both Pilzen and Klattau between March and October 1939 before it was called back to Germany and disbanded. However, in early 1941 after being re-formed it was relocated to Pilzen. The battalion would support local police units, but was weakened in strength as it was stretched across a comparatively large area. Despite this, by the spring of 1942 the battalion was enlarged to cover the districts of Tabor and Budweis.

In other parts of the Protectorate Order Police units continued to operate. The town of Jung-Bunzlau in north-eastern Bohemia was one of the oldest Jewish communities. Here Police Battalion *Jung-Bunzlau* was stationed. Following the creation of the Protectorate, it did not take long before the rights and freedoms of the Jewish inhabitants of the town and surrounding districts were curtailed. The repression of the Jews immediately grew into systematic anti-Jewish policy and this included the Order Police intimidating and persecuting them between March and October 1939. Later that year the battalion was called back to Germany and first partially and then completed disbanded.

In eastern Bohemia other Order Police units continued to cover large areas that also included Jewish communities. The towns of Pardubitz and Königgrätz were operated by Police Battalion *Pardubitz* from the autumn of 1939 until the summer of 1942. It was disbanded and absorbed by the Reserve Police Battalion *Kolin* in April 1942 which was located in Bohemia and was assigned as reinforcements to the police battalion garrisons at Jung-Bunzlau, Kolin, Königgrätz and Pardubitz following the assassination of Reinhard Heydrich.

During the weeks following the death of Heydrich, *Kolin* was given special duties such as carrying out death sentences passed by the SS as well as reprisal actions against suspected individuals and communities that were allegedly involved in the assassination of the *Reichsprotektor*. In fact there were 173 executions carried out between 3 June and 9 July 1942. These killings also took place in the hamlet of Ležáky, which was razed to the ground in a similar action taken against the village of Lidice.

In southern Bohemia various local district police and auxiliaries were supported by Police Battalion *Tábor*. It covered areas of the town of Tábor and was enlarged to include Budweis. The battalion operated between March and October 1939 and was then transferred to Prague. By April 1942 it was disbanded and absorbed by the Reserve Police Battalion *Klattau*.

Further east in Bohemia was Police Battalion *Iglau*. It was another police unit that operated between March and October 1939 and was then transferred to Poland in 1941. By April 1942 it was transferred to Norway, disbanded and absorbed by the Reserve Police Battalion *Holleschau*.

Some 100 miles east of Iglau in the town of Brunn was stationed Police Battalion *Brunn*. It operated between March and October 1939 and part of the battalion then transferred to Iglau during the summer of 1941. One company was moved to Slovenia, and a year later another company was sent to Russia and later disbanded.

In Moravia in the ancient town of Holleschau another police battalion was stationed and known as the Police Battalion *Holleschau*. It operated between March and October 1939 and was eventually disbanded by April 1941.

Apart from the territory of Bohemia and Moravia, the Order Police were garrisoned in numerous other occupied countries. The Baltic States included various *Volksdeutsche* (ethnic Germans) who were trained and recruited in June 1941 into various police units. These were known as *Ostland* police. The training of the police volunteers was under the control of the *Waffen-SS*. The recruits were sent to Berlin for training and by July 1941 some 400 Estonians and Estonian *Volksdeutsche* were assembled. Some 200 Latvian and Latvian *Volksdeutsche* were recruited under the command of *Hauptmann* August Hanner. Both the Estonian and Latvian police units were ethnically separated so there was no confusion. By August 1941 they were finally formed into what was known as the Police Reserve Battalion *Ostland*. Although they comprised mainly Estonian and Latvian police, ordinary German police were part of the battalion as well.

Training of these men was quite labour-intensive and prolonged and it was not until October 1941 that the battalion was transferred to the Soviet Union. Its area of operation was in the Ukraine and it reached Lwów on 10 October and then entered the Ukraine. Its existence as an *Ostland* police battalion was relatively short-lived as the Latvian company joined Police Battalion 320 and the Estonian Police Battalion 304.

Between 1939 and 1942 throughout the Reich, occupied countries and areas of military operations where German forces were still fighting, numerous police battalions were either disbanded or absorbed into other police units. In spite of these constant changes, the Order Police continued to be involved in guard duties, civil protection, road security, anti-airborne patrols, air-raid protection, anti-smuggling, black-market operations, mopping-up of Russian stragglers, armed escorts of freight transports, guarding, deporting, arrests and general policing duties in the occupied areas attached to the *Einsatzgruppen* and German army fighting units or were simply transferred into what was now known as the 4th *SS-Polizei* Panzer Division. The Order Police were garrisoned in a host of countries including France, Norway, Italy, the Netherlands, Belgium, Yugoslavia, Croatia and Slovenia where it undertook anti-partisan operations.

Although during this early period of the war the SS and police functioned as separate entities, by the summer of 1942 as the war on the Eastern Front continued to be fought it was decided that the Order Police would slowly be absorbed into the ranks of the *Waffen-SS* or turned into new SS Police Regiments. These new SS formations performed similar roles to the Order Police, but were often better armed. Their roles included security, anti-partisan actions and supporting *Waffen-SS* units on the Eastern Front. Separate police units still operated in all theatres, but these were military police of the Wehrmacht and were totally separate from duties performed by the Order Police.

By 1943 the division between the SS and the Order Police had virtually disappeared. SS officers then began to command police troops and police generals serving in command of soldiers were approved equal SS rank in the *Waffen-SS*.

The Order Police can be seen here marching along a road in France in 1940. The Order Police had grown to 244,500 men by mid-1940. Generally in France these men had multiple tasks such as checking movements and papers, and overseeing the French forces of order as they surrendered. They were also chiefly responsible for monitoring sensitive points, the primary communication infrastructure and the German internment camps. Numerous police units along with local police personnel also assisted in the round-ups, evacuation and escort of French Jews to stations where they were transported to concentration camps.

A captured French Colonial soldier accepting a cigarette from an Order Policeman following the capitulation of French forces in France in June 1940.

(**Above**) A photograph of an Order Policeman in France in 1940. During the last days of the war on the Western Front against France in June 1940 the Order Police was tasked with protecting the lines of communication and captured industrial facilities. This also included what was known as the 'combat of criminal elements and all political elements' that might threaten the occupation.

(**Opposite, above**) Wehrmacht and Order Policemen at a soup wagon in Lille. These policemen probably belonged to Police Battalion 62 which moved to France in October 1940. The Order Police also operated in France under Organization Todt (OT) which was located at fourteen different sites across France, Belgium and up to the Netherlands coast. In particular they were ordered to guard the U-boat facilities that were being constructed at Lorient, Saint-Nazaire and Brest. They were also tasked with guarding OT workers at the yards.

(**Opposite, below**) Police Chief Kurt Daluege reviewing troops in Luxembourg 1940. Following the invasion of Poland in October 1939, Police Battalion 123 was mobilized and sent to Luxembourg as its first operational area.

Caserne Negrier
Senkingwerk Hildesheim

(**Above**) Order Policemen can be seen here rounding up a group of people following a security action. In 1940 the Nazis more or less immediately outlawed all socialist and communist parties in the Netherlands. Consequently the Order Police undertook a series of security actions in order to round up those considered to be hostile opponents of the German occupation. The Jewish community was also targeted. Immediately following the occupation of the Netherlands, the German authorities implemented anti-Semitic measures. Between July and November 1940 Jewish citizens were expelled from public offices. By January 1941, Jewish civil servants had been removed from their jobs without further pay and Jewish people were no longer treated as members of society.

(**Opposite, above**) Order Police including local police auxiliaries rounding up Jews during a series of pogroms launched by governmental forces under Marshal and Conducător Ion Antonescu in the Romanian city of Iași which lasted from 29 June to 6 July 1941. According to Romanian authorities more than 13,266 people or one-third of the Jewish population were murdered in the pogrom itself and many others were deported.

(**Opposite, below**) Jews assembling in the courtyard of police headquarters during the Iași pogrom.

(**Above**) Jews are forced to clean blood from the cobblestone pavement of the Iași police headquarters courtyard during the pogrom.

(**Opposite**) Jews assembled by Romanian police and soldiers during the Iași pogrom sitting among corpses in the courtyard of the city police headquarters. There was at least one German police regiment present in the town during the time of the killings and was involved in the massacres with both Romanian officials and military units.

(**Below**) Romanian soldiers and police laying against the wall of police headquarters. The surviving Jews on the right are proceeding towards the train station from which they would be deported.

Jewish men sitting on the ground with shovels in Lithuania are guarded by an Order Policeman.

Deputy Reich Protector of Bohemia and Moravia and SS General Kurt Daluege practising with a Luger pistol, probably in Prague in 1942.

Kurt Daluege can be seen speaking in the centre, with Karl Hermann Frank on the right and Emil Hácha seated on the left, Prague, Czechoslovakia, September 1942.

(**Above**) In Prague *SS-Reichsführer* Heinrich Himmler along with Reinhard Heydrich on his right taking the salute to *Waffen-SS* troops. Heydrich was a high-ranking SS and police official and the main architect of the Holocaust. He was chief of the Reich Main Security office and acting Reich Protector of Bohemia and Moravia.

(**Opposite, above**) Heydrich and *SS-Obergruppenführer* Karl Hermann Frank taking the salute in Prague. Frank had great power in the protectorate. He controlled not only Nazi police apparatus in the Protectorate but the Gestapo, the SD and the Kripo as well. It was Frank who was instrumental in initiating the destruction of the Czech villages of Lidice and Ležáky in order to wreak revenge on the Czech populace for Heydrich's death.

(**Opposite, below**) On 10 June 1942 the Order Police were involved in the reprisal action at Lidice following the assassination of *Reichsprotektor* Reinhard Heydrich. The reprisal action saw the complete destruction of the village, the execution of 173 male inhabitants and the deportation of the women to Ravensbrück and the children to Łódź. In this photograph the buildings are being blown up.

Two photographs showing German police surveying the bodies of the men of Lidice executed within the grounds of the Horak farm. In the weeks following the death of Heydrich the Order Police began a wave of repressive measures by taking aggressive action against the inhabitants of Prague. Many companies were mobilized from numerous police administrations of the Reich and sent to Bohemia and Moravia.

Officers standing among the rubble of Lidice during the demolition of the town's ruins. The village was set on fire and the remains of the buildings destroyed with explosives. All the animals in the village including pets were shot as well. Himmler wanted every part of the village to disappear and this even included those buried in the town cemetery. The remains were dug up, looted for gold fillings and jewellery and then destroyed. A 100-strong German work party was later sent in to remove all visible remains of the village and re-route the stream running through it and also the roads. They then covered the entire site of the village with topsoil and planted crops.

Members of Police Battalion 323 and probably Lithuanian auxiliaries in front of the student dormitories of the University of Kaunas. *(United States Holocaust Memorial Museum – USHMM, courtesy of Christopher Wutz)*

Two photographs showing members of Police Battalion 323 receiving and packing up new equipment and clothing. This photograph was probably taken in Tilsit in Lithuania. This battalion undertook various actions against civilians in the summer of 1941 and was tasked with the surveillance of the Kaunas Ghetto.

Members of Police Battalion 323 march in a street in Tilsit. *(United States Holocaust Memorial Museum – USHMM)*

A Police Battalion 101 convoy of trucks assembly point at Moorwidenstrasse in Hamburg following air-raids. *(United States Holocaust Memorial Museum – USHMM)*

Five photographs showing Jewish deportees carrying a few personal belongings in bundles and suitcases marching through town from the assembly centre at the Platz'scher Garten to the railway station.

In the town of Würzburg, Germany, local SS men and Order Police can be seen rounding up Jews prior to their deportation in April 1942.

Police Sergeant Josef Herkert standing outside a building, probably in Würzburg.
(United States Holocaust Memorial Museum – USHMM)

Under the surveillance of the Order Police four photographs showing local residents looking on as a group of Jewish deportees arrives at the Fränkischer Hof assembly centre during a deportation action in Kitzingen. *(United States Holocaust Memorial Museum – USHMM)*

Julius Englert

Julius Englert

A Jewish man looking at the camera during a deportation action. An Order Policeman can be seen standing nearby.

The first of two photographs showing both French and German police assisting in the deportation action of Marseille Jews between 22 and 24 January 1943.

The Marseille round-up was the systematic deportation of the Jews of Marseille. The operation consisted of the complete expulsion of an entire neighbourhood of 30,000 persons.

Appendix

Order Police Battalions

The Order Police battalions were battalion-sized military units operated by the *Ordnungspolizei* between 1939 and 1942. They were subordinate to the SS and deployed in areas of German-occupied Europe and also operated in the rear areas of Wehrmacht, *Waffen-SS* and *Einsatzgruppen* operations. They were responsible for numerous crimes assisting in military operations in the rear and killing thousands of Jews and others who were regarded were enemies of the Nazi State.

Police Battalions in Poland (September 1939)

Police Battalion I/1	Police Battalion II/2	Police Battalion I/5
Police Battalion II/1	Police Battalion III/3	Police Battalion I/6
Police Battalion III/1	Police Battalion IV/2	Police Battalion II/6
Police Battalion IV/1	Police Battalion V/2	Police Battalion III/6
Police Battalion V/1	Police Battalion I/3	Police Battalion IV/6 1–2
Police Battalion I/2	Police Battalion I/4	

Regular Police Battalions (October 1939 to July 1942)

Police Battalion 1	Police Battalion 31	Police Battalion 66
Police Battalion 2	Police Battalion 32	Police Battalion 67
Police Battalion 3	Police Battalion 33	Police Battalion 68
Police Battalion 4	Police Battalion 41	Police Battalion 69
Police Battalion 5	Police Battalion 42	Police Battalion 71
Police Battalion 6	Police Battalion 43	Police Battalion 72
Police Battalion 7	Police Battalion 44	Police Battalion 73
Police Battalion 8	Police Battalion 45	Police Battalion 74
Police Battalion 9	Police Battalion 51	Police Battalion 81
Police Battalion 10	Police Battalion 52	Police Battalion 82
Police Battalion 11	Police Battalion 53	Police Battalion 83
Police Battalion 12	Police Battalion 54	Police Battalion 84
Police Battalion 13	Police Battalion 55	Police Battalion 85
Police Battalion 14	Police Battalion 56	Police Battalion 207
Police Battalion 21	Police Battalion 61	Police Battalion 208
Police Battalion 22	Police Battalion 62	Police Battalion 209
Police Battalion 23	Police Battalion 63	Police Battalion 210
Police Battalion 25	Police Battalion 64	Police Battalion 251
Police Battalion 26	Police Battalion 65	Police Battalion 252

Police Battalion 253
Police Battalion 254
Police Battalion 256
Police Battalion 301
Police Battalion 302
Police Battalion 303
Police Battalion 304
Police Battalion 305
Police Battalion 306
Police Battalion 307
Police Battalion 308
Police Battalion 309
Police Battalion 310
Police Battalion 311
Police Battalion 312
Police Battalion 313
Police Battalion 314
Police Battalion 315
Police Battalion 316
Police Battalion 317
Police Battalion 318
Police Battalion 319
Police Battalion 320
Police Battalion 321
Police Battalion 322
Police Battalion 323
Police Battalion 324
Police Battalion 325

Regular Police Battalions in the Protectorate (October 1939 to July 1942)

Police Battalion *Prague*
Police Battalion *Klattau*
Police Battalion *Jung-Bunzlau*
Police Battalion *Pardubitz*
Police Battalion *Kolin*
Police Battalion *Tabor*
Police Battalion *Iglau*
Police Battalion *Brunn*
Police Battalion *Holleschau*
Police Battalion *Ostland*
Reserve Police Battalion *Leipzig*